D0855294

BATMAN & ROBIN

THE TRAIL OF TRICKS

Batman and Robin
Use Footwear and
Tire Tread Analysis
to Crack the Case

by Steve Korté
art by Dario Brizuela
Batman created by Bob Kane with Bill Finger

Consultants:
David Foran, PhD, and Katelyn Kranz, BS
Michigan State University
Forensic Science Graduate Program
East Lansing, Michigan

CAPSTONE PRESS
a capstone imprint

The Gotham City Zoo has been burglarized! Two rare animals have been stolen.

The police have arrived. They are questioning the workers at the zoo.

Police Commissioner Gordon has placed a call to Batman and Robin, asking them to help.

"I'll look for fingerprints on the door of the hyena's pen," says Robin.

"Good idea, Robin," replies Batman. "I'll search the area just outside the pen."

Robin removes a small metal container and a brush from his Utility Belt. He opens the container and dips the brush into a black powder. Then he lightly dusts the handle on the door to the hyena's pen to search for fingerprints.

"All the prints on this handle overlap and are smudged, Batman," he calls out. "It looks like fingerprints won't help us solve this crime."

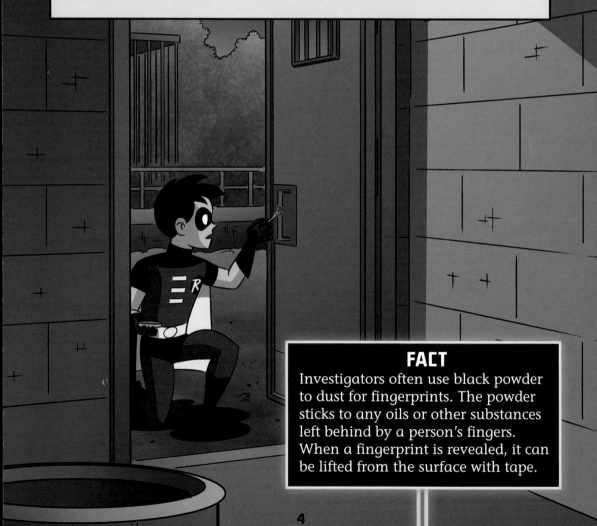

FACT
Investigators often use black powder to dust for fingerprints. The powder sticks to any oils or other substances left behind by a person's fingers. When a fingerprint is revealed, it can be lifted from the surface with tape.

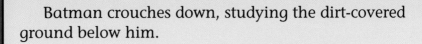

Batman crouches down, studying the dirt-covered ground below him.

"No luck here either," says Batman. "I'm afraid the police and zookeepers have trampled the area. There are no usable shoe prints."

"Why are you looking for those?" Robin asks.

"Shoe prints can help us identify the type of shoe the thief was wearing," says Batman. "If we find a shoe print here, we can compare its pattern to the bottom of a suspect's shoe."

Batman and Robin move to the front of the zoo. The giant metal gate is still wide open. The wires for the zoo's security camera system have been cut.

Batman studies the muddy area just inside the zoo's entrance.

"What are you looking for?" asks Robin.

"I'm looking for a certain pattern of shoe print on the ground," says Batman.

"You mean what direction the shoe prints are facing?" asks Robin.

"Not exactly," says Batman. "I have a theory about the shoe prints in the mud over here. There was no forced entry into the zoo. I suspect the thief climbed over the wall."

FACT

Investigators study the pattern of ridges, curves, squares, and lines made by the bottom of a shoe. These details can reveal the shoe's brand. Also, any nicks or cuts found within those patterns can be compared to a suspect's shoe.

"Oh, I get, it," says Robin. "You're looking for shoe prints that suddenly appear in the middle of this muddy area, with no matching prints behind them. That could mean that someone jumped from a height and landed in the mud."

"Yes," says Batman. "And after climbing over the wall, the thief destroyed the security system and stole the hyenas . . ."

". . . and then opened the gate of the zoo from the inside to escape," adds Robin.

FACT
Footprints and shoe prints that can be seen with the naked eye are called visible prints. They are created when a person steps into mud, blood, paint, or some other substance.

Batman and Robin carefully search the muddy ground.

"Batman, look over here!" says Robin. "These two shoe prints in the middle are different than any of the prints that are closer to the wall. And what is that grainy material next to the two prints?"

"Good eye, Robin," says Batman. "You can get some photos of those prints, then I'll collect a soil sample."

Robin reaches into his Utility Belt and says, "I've got my micro camera here."

"We're also going to need a tripod and a light," says Batman. "You'll find them in the Batmobile."

FACT
Stepping into a soft surface, such as mud, snow, or dirt, leaves behind a 3-D impression called a plastic print.

Robin positions the tripod and camera directly over one of the shoe prints. Batman sets up a lamp at an angle that shines a bright light onto the print.

"That's called oblique lighting," says Batman. "The light casts a shadow on the shoe print, so we'll be able to see more details and the depth of the ridges when we view your photos."

Robin takes photos of the shoe prints, and then he asks, "Now what?"

"After I've collected a sample of the grainy material, we'll create casts, or 3-D models, of the shoe prints," says Batman.

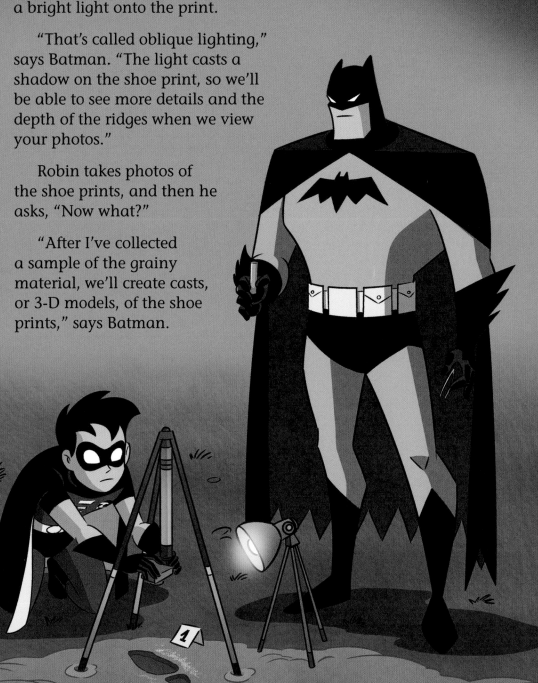

After Batman collects a soil sample, he hands Robin a plastic bag and bottle of water. The plastic bag contains a fine gray powder.

"Mix the powder and water together in this bag," says Batman. "It will create dental stone."

Soon Robin holds a bag filled with a thick liquid.

"Now pour the dental stone along the side of the shoe prints," says Batman. "Allow it to slowly fill the entire area."

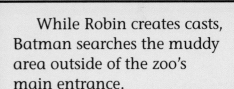

While Robin creates casts, Batman searches the muddy area outside of the zoo's main entrance.

"Come take a look at some interesting impressions in the mud over here," Batman calls out to Robin.

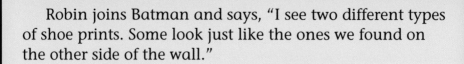

Robin joins Batman and says, "I see two different types of shoe prints. Some look just like the ones we found on the other side of the wall."

"That's right," says Batman. "And the other shoe prints are much smaller, with no ridges."

"So that could mean there were two people involved in this burglary," says Robin. "Looks like I need to get a few more photos and casts."

FACT
Shoe prints can give clues about a person's movement. Investigators can sometimes tell if a person was running, based on the space between the prints.

While Robin pours dental stone into the shoe prints, Batman stares at the ground, deep in thought.

"I would like you to make one more cast," Batman says. "Let's get a cast of these tire tracks in the dirt road."

"Tire tracks?" asks Robin. "What can those tell us about the crime?"

"The thieves probably used a getaway vehicle," says Batman. "Tire treads can identify a tire's manufacturer and date of release. Sometimes they even tell us the type of vehicle a suspect used."

"And what happens if we find a vehicle we believe the suspects used?" asks Robin.

"We examine the vehicle's tires to see if one of them matches the same pattern of grooves and ridges found in this tire track," says Batman. "And if there is anything unique about the tread, like uneven wear or nicks or cuts, we can try to match it to the tire on a suspect's vehicle."

"I guess we need more photos and another cast," says Robin as he reaches for his camera.

"That's right," says Batman.

14

"It takes about thirty minutes for dental stone to fully harden," says Batman. "The shoe print casts should be ready to remove."

Robin uses the edge of a knife to lift the shoe print casts out of the ground. He carries them carefully to the area in front of the zoo.

Batman studies the tire track as Robin fills it with dental stone.

"Based on the width of this track, and the number of shoe prints we've found, we're probably looking for two suspects who were riding a motorcycle," Batman says.

After thirty minutes, Robin removes the tire track casts from the ground.

15

Batman and Robin carry the casts of the shoe prints and tire track over to the Batmobile.

"Let's go, Robin," says Batman as he jumps into the Batmobile. "It's time to do some lab work in the Batcave."

"And solve this crime!" adds Robin.

The Batmobile heads toward the outskirts of Gotham City. Suddenly, Batman makes a sharp turn onto a deserted dirt road that leads to the hidden entrance to the Batcave.

"Time to use the anti-tracker," says Batman.

Robin leans forward to press a red button on the dashboard.

WHOOSH!

A powerful air blower on the back of the car erases the Batmobile's tire tracks from the dusty road.

"There's no chance of anyone following our tire tracks," says Robin with a smile.

In the Batcave, Batman studies the casts of the tire tracks and the shoe prints.

Robin uploads the photos from the crime scene into the Batcomputer. He enlarges the shoe print photos so that they fill the screen.

After a few minutes Robin says, "I found a match for one of the shoes, Batman. There was a logo etched on the sole of the larger shoe print. The Batcomputer matched it to a men's dress shoe manufactured by a small company in England. I couldn't find any information on the smaller shoe print."

"I've studied the shoe print casts," says Batman. "There's a chunk missing from the heel of one of the larger shoes."

"According to the Batcomputer's database, the tire track pattern matches a tire manufactured for an Italian motorcycle," Robin says. "It was only produced four years ago."

"Good work, Robin," says Batman. "Now I'm going to do a little soil analysis."

Batman reaches for the vial containing the grainy material that he collected at the crime scene.

FACT

Investigators usually look at photos in catalogs or reach out to tire companies in order to compare vehicle tires and tire tread patterns. These tire patterns include lines, curves, zigzags, diamonds, waves, and blocks.

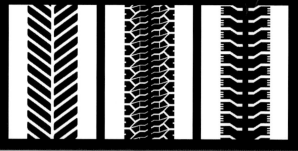

"After I get this sample ready, I'm going to place it inside this ICP-MS machine," he says. "That stands for inductively coupled plasma mass spectrometry. The machine will analyze the soil."

A few minutes later, Robin reads the data from the machine.

"Batman, the soil contains almost all silica," he says. "That's sand, right?"

"That's right, Robin," says Batman. "When one of our suspects jumped from the front wall of the zoo, there's a chance that some sand fell from his shoes or pants cuffs."

"I've got an idea who our two suspects might be," says Robin. "You know that deserted amusement park on Gotham Harbor's beach?" Robin says.

"Yes, what about it?" asks Batman.

"It's the perfect hideout for the Joker and his girlfriend, Harley Quinn." Robin says. "They both escaped from Arkham Asylum last week."

"Good thinking, Robin," says Batman. "They probably drove to the zoo on the Joker's motorcycle. Harley may have helped lift the Joker over the wall."

"That would explain the shoe prints that appeared in the mud inside the zoo's wall," says Robin.

"There's one more clue we can learn from the shoe prints," says Batman. "The last time we fought the Joker, I threw a Batarang at him that broke off part of the heel on his left shoe. That could match the damaged heel on one of the shoe print casts."

"Come on, Robin," says Batman. "Now that we've retraced the Joker's and Harley's footsteps, let's pay a visit to their hideout."

Batman and Robin jump into the Batmobile. Soon, they screech to a halt outside the broken-down Gotham Amusement Park. The Dynamic Duo crash through the wooden door of the Fun House.

The Joker and Harley Quinn look up with surprise. Next to them are the two hyena cubs.

"Come on, Harley!" yells the Joker. "Let's give our guests a proper welcome!"

The Joker and Harley Quinn jump onto the Joker's motorcycle.

VROOOOM!

With an evil grin on his face, the Joker steers the vehicle straight toward Batman and Robin.

"Let's see how they look wearing tire treads on top of their capes!" says the Joker with a laugh.

Just before the Joker's motorcycle hits Robin, the Boy Wonder leaps and somersaults out of the way.

Batman throws a roped Batarang into the air. The long rope loops around the two villains and yanks them off the cycle. They hit the ground with a thud.

Robin tosses a net over the frightened hyenas to keep them from running away. Batman ties the two villains tightly together.

"This is all your fault, Harley," grumbles the Joker. "You just had to have hyenas for pets, didn't you?"

"What's going to happen to my babies?" Harley demands angrily.

Don't worry, Harley. The hyenas will be safe at the zoo very soon.

And for stepping out of line, the two of you will be making tracks straight back to Arkham Asylum!

MORE ABOUT FOOTWEAR AND TIRE TREAD ANALYSIS

- Criminals sometimes wear gloves to avoid leaving fingerprints. However, they rarely think to disguise their footwear.

- The famous fictional detective Sherlock Holmes said, "There is no branch of detective science which is so important and so much neglected as the art of tracing footsteps."

- Footwear evidence should be one of the first items to be investigated at a crime scene. Unfortunately, footwear evidence is often damaged by the police and other people stepping on top of it.

- Although two people may buy the same brand of shoes, the wear patterns on the bottom of their shoes can help identify a suspect. Investigators also look for any damage to the ridges and grooves of a shoe, such as tears or missing chunks.

- Shoe prints can help investigators determine the steps a person took while committing a crime and leaving a crime scene.

- A shoe print that is hard to see with the naked eye is called a latent print. Special lights and powders can help to reveal latent prints.

- Investigators study tire marks to determine what happened at traffic accidents. Skid marks can help reveal how fast a vehicle was traveling or the direction it traveled leaving the scene. This can help determine who was at fault in an accident.

- In a hit-and-run crime, a driver hits someone or something with his or her vehicle and drives away without reporting an accident. However, the tire marks left behind can sometimes provide enough clues to lead investigators to the vehicle.

GLOSSARY

analyze (AN-uh-lize)—to examine something carefully in order to understand it

cast (KAST)—a model of an object, sometimes in plaster; casts show details of the original object

database (DAY-tuh-bays)—a collection of organized information on a computer

evidence (EV-uh-duhnss)—information, items, and facts that help prove something to be true or false

hyena (hy-EE-nuh)—a large omnivore that lives in Africa and Asia

impression (im-PRESH-uhn)—a mark or design produced by pressing or stamping

oblique (oh-BLEEK)—at an angle

ridge (RIJ)—a narrow raised strip

silica (SIL-uh-kah)—a chemical found in sand

theory (THEE-ur-ee)—an idea that explains something that is unknown

tread (TRED)—a series of bumps and grooves used for grip or traction, such as on a shoe or tire

READ MORE

Carmichael, L. E. *Discover Forensic Science*. What's Cool about Science? Minneapolis: Lerner Publications, 2017.

Kawa, Katie. *Forensic Detectives*. Out of the Lab: Extreme Jobs in Science. New York: PowerKids Press, 2016.

Orr, Tamra B. *Investigating a Crime Scene*. Follow the Clues. Ann Arbor, Mich.: Cherry Lake Publishing, 2014.

INTERNET SITES

Use FactHound to find Internet sites related to this book.
Visit *www.facthound.com*
Just type in 9781515768579 and go.

INDEX

OTHER TITLES IN THIS SET

DNA ANALYSIS

FIRE INVESTIGATION

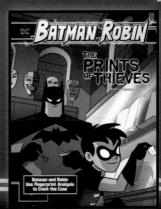

FINGERPRINT ANALYSIS

Published by Capstone Press in 2017
1710 Roe Crest Drive
North Mankato, Minnesota 56003
www.mycapstone.com

Copyright © 2017 DC Comics
BATMAN and all related characters and elements are
trademarks of and © DC Comics.
(s17)
STAR38590

All rights reserved. No part of this publication may be reproduced in whole or in part, or
stored in a retrieval system, or transmitted in any form or by any means, electronic, mechanical,
photocopying, recording, or otherwise, without written permission of the publisher.

Cataloging-in-publication information is on file with the Library of Congress.
ISBN: 978-1-5157-6857-9 (library binding)
ISBN: 978-1-5157-6870-8 (eBook PDF)

Summary: Batman and Robin use footwear and tire tread analysis techniques to solve a burglary
at the Gotham City Zoo.

Editorial Credits
Christopher Harbo, editor; Brann Garvey, designer; Tori Abraham, production specialist

Illustration Credits
Luciano Vecchio, back cover, 1, 32

Printed in the United States of America.
010364F17